MW01679774

Carroll's Collections

From the Heart

By Carroll Dean Stephens Coleman, B.S., MEd.

2011

Editing and Design – Daniel R. Coleman, DBA
Publisher – Cowboy Book Works and Loaded Dice Publishing
ISBN – 978-09823158-6-6

"All rights reserved. No part of this publication may be reproduced, stored in a retrieval system, or transmitted, in any form or by any means, electronic, mechanical, photocopying, recording, or otherwise, without the written prior permission of the author."

Contact the author through
Cowboybookworks@yahoo.com or visit
www.readreedbooks.com

Carroll Dean Stephens Coleman

Carroll Dean Stephens was born March 12, 1933, in Temple Texas. Carroll was the fourth child born to William Carroll Stephens and Edith Margaret Smith. Other children of the family, Jim (deceased), Margaret, Jane (deceased), Robert and Myra were all born in Texas.

Carroll grew up in Temple, and graduated from Temple High School, in 1950, and received her Associate of Arts degree from Temple Jr. College, in 1952. She married Larry D. Coleman on September 20, 1952, in San Marcos, Texas. Carroll received her B.S. degree in elementary education, from Southwest Texas State Teachers College in 1956, and her, Master of education degree, from McMurry College, in Abilene, Texas, in 1965. She completed an additional 45 semester hours of graduate work at Indiana State University.

Carroll taught in the private and public schools of Texas, Oklahoma, Arkansas, and Indiana. She retired in 1995, after completing her 40th year of classroom instruction. During her teaching career, Carroll received numerous awards and honors, for outstanding teaching. She was very active in state and local professional and educational organizations, and a member of the American Association of University Women.

Carroll is the mother of three children, Debra, David, and Daniel. She has seven grandchildren, two step-grandchildren, and one great grandchild.

Some of Carroll's poems, prayers, thoughts, and reflections are provided in this publication. Some of her work has been published in journals, newspapers and books. She continues to enjoy her writing and crafts, and being a wife, mother, grandmother, and great grandmother. She and her husband are members of the Lakewood United Methodist Church, in Houston, Texas.

A LOVE POEM TO THE WORLD

It is beautiful to be alive and loved.
I have been blessed from God above
With a wonderful man, three lovely children,
Two darling grand babies, and many a friend.
To love and be loved is very, very special
In my world today are many nice people.
Thank you, Dear Lord,
For my world of love, so true and so fine!

Carroll Dean Stephens Coleman
1983

Dedicated to my family and friends for all their love and support.

Contents

1 On Family

Words of Love for Larry

Come my Love and sit with me
Think back on yesterday—
When we were young
We longed to be in each other's arms
We became one and years have passed
Some gray hair we can see
But still my love
We long to be in each others arms.
Would we change the way we feel
Or any of our love
Not today or yesterday
For we have found true love.

How Do I Love Thee, Larry

How do I love thee?
I don't know how to tell
As much as it takes to fill the deepest well
As long as it takes to travel
The world around more than twice
As big as the tallest mountain
Reaching high into the sky
As wide as the ocean
When measured from side to side
I love you with my heart, body, mind and soul
More than ever could be told!

Cooking for My Sweetie

Chocolate cookies
Chocolate hearts
Red jello and lemon tarts
Chocolate cake
Chocolate pies
Cherry cobbler and chicken fried
I've made these all for my true love
And kept him home like a turtle dove.

Father

F is for the faith he taught me.
A is for all he did for us kids.
T is for the times he bounced me on his knee.
H is for his heart that had no lid.
E is for his twinkling eyes of blue.
R is for right and right as he could be.

Put them all together they spell Father
God gave the sweetest one to me.

My Mother

My mother was lovable because she was so kind.
My mother was a great cook, and a seamstress so fine.
My mother was a good nurse and took good care of us.
We children loved her and miss her very much.

My Father's Path

I was my father's namesake
And proud of it for sure.
I was his little shadow
Running to make the tour.
His steps were very big,
My legs were very short,
He would often hold my hand
Pulling me from the start.
Sometimes I would skip and hop
Not to be left behind
Moving as fast as I could
With two steps at a time.

A Song for Father

Fathers are strong and wise.
They help us in many ways.
Their guidance and patience
Help us endure the days
With heartaches and despair.

Fathers are playful and fun.
They teach us to give and share.
Their arms protect us from harm
Through their love we learn to care
For others in despair.

My Mother's Heart

There was nothing, but love in my mother's heart.
She worked from early dawn until past dark.
All children minded her and she was love by everyone.
She raised eleven siblings, four daughters and two sons.
My mother's beauty was natural, she wore no make-up
Unless my sisters and I gave her facial and the such.
I remember one time when my dad made a date
To take her to a movie, said they wouldn't be late.
So we girls all got busy and made Mama up so fine.
Daddy was so proud of his best girl—she looked sublime!
He smiled and winked when they went out the door
We thought they looked younger than they ever had before.

My Mother's Eyes

My mother's eyes were soft and gray.
Her expression was always caring.
She didn't have time to sit and hold us,
But the love in her eyes—never left us doubting.
If one of us kids ever got sick
She sat close—her eyes ever watching,
She would close her eyes only to pray,
To ask God for our rapid healing.

If my mother had to correct us
With punishment—like a spanking,
Her loving eyes shed tears, just like ours.
She would say her heart was breaking!
It wasn't 'til I had children of my own
That I knew what she was feeling.
I'll always remember my mother's eyes,

Which made her love so revealing.
The vision of her beautiful eyes
Is in my mind and heart for safe keeping.
Mother's Day 2007

My Mama's Flower Garden

My Mama's flower garden was a beautiful sight to see!
Every color under the sun was captured for our ecstasy.
There were hollyhocks in splendor, piercing purple to the skies,
And lovely lilac bushes, curving mounds to meet our eyes.

Black-eyed Susans gently swaying, golden with centers dark,
A thick row of zinnias splashing colors of all sorts.
There were sweet peas and sweet Williams, casting shades of pink and rose.
Oh! Our eyes welcome the radiance, as the aroma filled each nose.

Mama knew just when to plant them, and how to make them grow.
She watered and she trimmed them and commanded some in rows.
Mama's garden was like a shining sea with rolling waves of color.
Each beauty given time to bloom, never cheating one another.

Every specie had a spectacular hue—
So many, many flowers—I only named a few!
And I know today in Heaven that God's garden is so fair,
Because my Mama helps to tend His beautiful flowers with great care.
1983

Ties to My Father

My ties to my father was a close one
For my name was the same as his.
I often accompanied my Dad
Wherever he went
To keep up, he'd hold my hand, as I ran.
I was one of his six children
But his name was given to me.
I love the name that I go by,
But it often caused problems for me.
The spelling is not for a female
Carroll is the spelling for a man.
Ties for Dad meant special occasions
Like weddings, funerals, and church.
These were ties---around his neck,
But the tie that he wore everyday
Was his love that was tied to our hearts?

A Song for Mothers

A mother's love never dies
From the cradle to the grave.
She loves her children
All her life
And cares for them without much strife.

A mother's love is not enough
She must raise her children
So others can love them, too.
When she's gone
Her love through them continues on.

Pop, My Dad

I always called my Dad, "Pop."
He didn't seem to mind
Or if he did, he never said.
Maybe he was just too kind.
My Pop loved us very much,
And he worked very hard
To keep us clothed
And reminded each of us
To pray when he tucked us into bed.

My Great Grandmother

My great grandmother was Irish
It was very plain to see
Her eyes were green
Her hair was red
And her name was Rosalee.

Great grandmother came from Ireland
By boat from far away
Many years ago
Her smile was like sunshine
And her heart was good as gold!

A Great Day

January 23, 1954 was a great day for a baby, a daddy, a mama-me.
It was cold, but the sun was bright—I remember it well!
God sent to us a baby girl.
The softest thing I every held!
Our relatives all came to see

The prettiest baby in the nursery, in Temple, Texas, on Avenue G.
As parents, so very proud and young,
We thanked the Lord for our little one,
And gave her the name of Debra Lou.
January 24, 1954

October 28

On October 28 in 1957
Our lives were touched again.
A baby boy was sent to us—
Another gift from heaven.
Strong in statute—
Sweet in nature—
His name was given—David
His sister then had a brother.
We brought him home
With a band playing
In San Marcos, Texas.
So proud to have another child
Another little Coleman.

Our Third Baby

In Abilene, on Labor Day
On September 4 in 1960,
We had a great surprise,
Another precious baby.
We named him Daniel Reed
And to God we gave thanks.
He weighed 8 pounds and 9 ounces,
And was 22 inches in length.
He had blue eyes and was as handsome as could be.
He was a happy baby, and seldom seemed to cry.
He was absolutely perfect, to his parents, Larry and I.

Now our family has 3 D's,
Debra, David, and Daniel.
God give us guidance to raise them right,
To teach them to love you,
And to say their prayers each night!
September 30, 1960.

Five Decades of Marriage

We said our "I dos" in '52.
And began our life as "man and wife"
Our college years were postponed
In '54—Debra came along.

She was a beautiful baby girl
With big blue eyes and blonde bouncing curls
Was quick to learn and loved to read
Liked to do things independently.

We were so young—yet determined
To get degrees and our education
Life was hard, but we didn't know
Because we loved each other so!

We went to the windy west
To teach and give it our very best
Three promotions were quite a shock
Millersview, Sterling City, and Paint Rock.

As educators we made progress
Back to our home in San Marcos
In '57 our family grew
God sent Dave, in a bundle in blue.

David was a good-looking lad
A sweet disposition—seldom got mad
Strong in character and leadership
Thought of others before himself.

We spent three years at SMA
Next we ventured West again by fate
Back where sand and tumbleweed blew
In Abilene trying to make dreams come true.

In '60 we were blessed again
With another boy, who we named Dan
A decade came and quickly passed
How could ten years go so fast.

Dan our third child was such a joy
He was bright, handsome little boy
Tennis and Scout honors he gained
Was quiet, thoughtful—never complained

Deb, Dave, and Dan were our three D's
Each minded their parents and tried to please
They did well in school—made us so proud
All three stood out among the crowds.

One half of our second decade elapsed
On Westview Drive in a two-story house
We were a happy family
Living our lives in harmony.

With two degrees in each our hands
We left Texas—bound for Sooner land
A doctorate this time—was our goal
Our future's destiny to unfold.

Three full years of dedication
'68 brought celebration
Dr. Coleman was Larry's title
A salutation with satisfaction.

Off we went as a caravan
And we settled down in Razorback land
Our three D's adjusted quite well
Good lives in Conway to compel.

Three years in a small town setting
Teaching, learning, playing, and growing
All five Coleman's loved Arkansas
But none liked the Razorback call.

New jobs to a land of cold
To a strange sounding town—we didn't know
To Terre Haute, Indiana
Winter clothes were an "extravaganza."

We endured new things in '71
For each different lives had begun
New school, new jobs, new friends, new climate
It was hard, but we made it.

Two hearts danced as one in '72
Two decades ended with love renewed
Life was hard, but we didn't know
Because we loved each other so!

The seventies were challenging years
Advancing and preparing our careers
There was dating, dancing, driving

Three teens loving parents supervising.

High school and college graduates
Our three D's advanced their education
They studied and worked to pass each test
They made good grades and did their best.

Our three D's got BA's from IU
To Kappa Sig and Chi O they were true
Two D's got MBA's
And Dave got a CLU.

In seventy-seven, we bought an acre
Which became quite an adventure
We really planned to build later
But couldn't wait the endeavor.

We sold our house in Lincolnshire
And moved to a hotel for a while
Larry began to cut down trees
On the lot where our home would be.

Ground was broken in mid-July
Were told we'd be in for pumpkin pie
October and November passed
We left a rent house for Christmas—at last.

We loved our house on Avalon
A big English tudor by design
It was most fun on holidays
With all ten Coleman's there to play.

Five good years leading to '82
Thirty years end with 'much to do."

We made a trip to Tennessee
And saw OU beat Kentuckee.

We were so busy at this time
We were young and in our prime
Life was good and we didn't know
Because we loved each other so!

The eighties were lean, as I recall
The economy slowed for one and all
We all worked hard to do our best
Counting our blessings—forgetting the rest.

Eighty-six was especially rough
Larry's heart problem was really tough
Family and friends came to our aid
What comfort they were—as we prayed.

By the end of the fourth decade
There were many changes that were made
Five grandchildren had come along
The Coleman Clan was thirteen strong.

Twice a year we would congregate
All the Coleman group would celebrate
Everyone came at Christmas time
And met in July for summer sunshine.

Big events came with the nineties
Two more Coleman's came "pitter-patty"
We'd no idea in the fifties
That we would produce so many.

With the decade there was a crisis

Which turned out to be a blessing
A wreck changed our priorities
Made the choice to retire come easily.

We also bought some real estate
With four transactions to be exact
We sold a home and a condo
Bought two houses where snow doesn't blow.

The next five years were exciting
Much time was spent moving and packing
We finally got things situated
Both homes finished and decorated.

Friends and family wondered where
If we'd be here or would be there
We go when the spirit moves us
To the city or to the beaches.

God has always come first in our home.
Thanking Him wherever we roamed
Teaching our children never to lie, steal, or cheat
His constant love made our lives complete.

We come to the end of five decades
And we recall our vows we made
We eloped fifty years ago
Because we loved each other so!
March 20, 2002

Three Added Blessings

We can't forget three great blessings
That have been added through the seasons
Barbara is the first I'll name
A misplaced Hoosier that Texas claims.

David brought her from way up North
To a land of trucks and the sorts
A young bride in strange surroundings
She jumped right in and started teaching.

Her hard work and positive traits
Are a few things that make her great!
She's gentle, caring and pretty, too
May I introduce her to you.

Another blessing in our lives
Dan made Tammy Louise his wife
An import from New Mexico
Now she lives in San Antonio.

She plays a guitar and sings, too
Ask her and she will play for you
She's full of fun and lots of laughs
Sometimes her humor is a blast.

Tammy is friendly, helpful and kind
A true optimist all the time
She is beautiful and petite
A more loving person you'll never meet.

The third blessing which comes to mind
Is Craig Cordell a man so fine

He seems to love Deb very much
Is pleasant, patient and the such.

He's a tease with lots of humor
Once your friend, a friend forever
His clear blue eyes and pleasant smile
His cherry spirit lingers awhile.

At computers Craig is a whiz
He's also good at a sports quiz
If help you need, he's a handy man
Glad to have you in the Coleman clan.
July 15, 2002—Written for 50th wedding anniversary,
September 20, 2002.

Our Seven Grandchildren

Our first was born in seventy-eight
A baby boy who didn't make us wait
He made his appearance in the far Midwest
On July 14th, we learned we were blessed.

Craig Cullen was the name he was given
He had hazel eyes—hair that was flaxen
He was a beautiful boy—was loved by all
He talked and walked early, as I recall.

Our very first grandson is now a man
He is straight and tall with a handsome tan
With a wonderful smile and a charming way
Loved him yesterday and still do today.

In '81—came a dainty May flower
Arriving in Denver with spring snow showers

Christina Colleen was so soft and so sweet
A pretty baby from her head to her feet.

Christina's name was shortened to Chrissy
Sometimes called Princess, Sunshine or Missy
She has a twinkle in her eye and pearly white teeth
With satin smooth skin and is quite petite.

Our little soccer girl is all grown –up
Gone are the days when we played U-Haul trucks
She is a young woman in her college years
She's loved so very much and is so dear.

Our third blessing of joy came in '85
Another granddaughter so much alive
She was late in arriving for July 4th
But the next day in Houston marks her birth.

A beautiful pink baby with lots of hair
We first saw Elizabeth Nicole in her daddy's care
He was holding her and she looked at him as if to say
I'm glad to be here, it's been a long day.

Elizabeth was a happy little girl
So pretty and sweet with ribbon tied curls
We had fun at tea parties with dolls and bears
She's sweet seventeen now and oh so dear.

Austin DeMurr came in eighty-seven
Another blessing was sent from heaven
On June 6, from Houston, Texas a call came
To announce Austin's arrival to our "Hall of Fame."

Austin was a good natured baby boy

Was easy to care for—and such a joy
He had long eye lashes and big blue eyes
Entertained himself and seldom cried.

Austin participates in lots of sports
Golf, basketball, cross country and the sorts
His disposition is thoughtful, good and kind
A grandson that will be loved all the time.

A special present came in eighty-eight
On Christmas Day, in the afternoon late
Brian David said, "Hi" to our world in Michigan
He was our fifth grandchild and third grandson.

Brian was a happy baby and cute as a bug
He loved to get kisses and lots of hugs
Now he likes to tell jokes to make people laugh
Tell him a yarn and he'll tell you one back.

Sports cars, computer games, and e-mail too
All hold his interest which he'll share with you
Brian is a sweet boy with a tender heart
He knows that we have loved him from the start.

In 1990, in the month of July
Our sixth grandchild was named for a famous guy
He answers to Samuel Houston in old San Antonio
A finer lad you'll never want to know.

Sam is so smart with a curious mind
He has questions galore of every kind
He will make a successful lawyer, I am sure
Or become a doctor with a marvelous cure.

He is a great player at basketball
He swishes the basket when the ball falls
Another Sam Houston will make history
Our love for Sam will last an eternity.

Our last grandchild was a baby princess
She arrived in '95 and is so very precious
Katherine Corinne appeared in May
On the fourteenth which was Mother's Day.

A sweet little girl who likes to wear hats
Play dress-up and Barbies and things like that
She has long blonde curls, blue eyes and a giggle
She never sits still and is a constant wiggle.

She is smart as a whip and loves her books
She has lots of talent to go with her looks
Katie is her nickname and is loved by all
A blessing from heaven—mighty but small.

Seven grandchildren for which we are thankful
Seven lives for which we are responsible
The Coleman and Stephens lines to carry on
God help us to guide them to be true and strong.

We love each of them very, very much
Being together and keeping in touch
We treasure each moment when we are with them
We love each dearly and will to the end.
June 10, 2002—written for 50th Wedding Anniversary,
September 20, 2002.

Margaret, My Sister

M is for the *many* things she made for me.
A is for *always* lending me her car.
R is for helping Mom and Dad to *raise* me.
G is for her *good* advice which took me far.
A is for *aiding* me with projects.
R is for *rescue* when cash was low.
E is for *ever* love and friendship.
T is for our *telephones* which keep us close.

Put them all together—they spell *MARGARET,*
A sister—who means the world to me.

Written for Margaret Stephens Pagel on her 80th birthday, December 5, 2000.

Four Girl Cousins

Jacks, jump rope, and paper dolls
Movies, train trips, and summer time fun
Mary Jane, Billie Ann, Patsy and Carroll
Four loving cousins and happy little girls.

Each day brought a new adventure
What one couldn't think of—the others could capture
Whether they were in town or on the farm
The little girls' pledge to secrecy were scorn.

Janie, the oldest of the four,
Often wrote plays for them to perform
The movies inspired her to great heights
As they became mourners, Indians, or knights.

The artist was Billie Ann
With her talent and great imagination
They made settings with glue, paint, and paper
To them it seemed real—it didn't matter.

Patsy and Carroll just went along
Sometimes with regret if the truth were known
Like the time they were to cut their arms
To make a red man and pale face brothers—as one.

Once a movie on how airplanes fly
Convinced Janie that they should try
So up on the garage they climbed so high
Their bravery was not to be denied.

The flight controllers ordered the calls
For the cardboard flaps, skirt, cape and parasol
Rubber tires were stacked to prevent them from crashing
Three flights were cancelled with Patsy smashing.

The mothers of the girls were sisters
They would sometimes have to consider
To separate the four little cousins
For peace of mind and their protection.

Tears were shed when the girls couldn't play
Soon their mamas would give in and say
You girls must be careful whatever you do
Make us a promise and we'll believe you.

There were hugs and giggles at their reunion
And for a while there was no commotion
But soon the little girls' imaginations
Were in full swing with new anticipation.

They saw a movie once about Mexico
Janie decided that was where they should go
They tied their tooth brushes in red bandanas
And they headed south for old Mexicana.

Their destination was never reached
By the four little girls with their bare feet
About a mile down the railroad track
Billie Ann stepped on a piece of glass.

Billie Ann was crying and bleeding a lot
Janie took a bandana and tied a knot
Around Billie's leg which slowed the bleeding
And her instruction sent Patsy and Carroll a-running.

When they arrived at the filling station
They were gasping for breath with their explanation
They explained what happened but it was a task
Three jumped in a truck and hurried back to the track.

Janie acted as a doctor to help Billie mend
With the aid of two nurses at her command
They waited on Billie because she couldn't walk
It's been forgotten how many stitches the doctor took.

Another time when the girls played doctor
Was when the Christmas dolls took pneumonia
Each doll died like in a movie they saw
And with funerals were buried in the back yard.

The little girls didn't mean to ruin their dolls
But it rained for quite a while
When the brand new dolls were retrieved

Their pretty faces were stained with rain.

Now when the cousins were on the farm
They were kept busy doing the chores
There were eggs to gather and wood to fetch
There were beans to snap and peaches to pick.

When the jobs were done and it was time to play
They swam in the river and rolled in the hay
They rode horses or played with the cats
Or swung on the grape vines and things like that.

The four little girls would wish on the stars
And played slinging statues on the boulevard
They grew up and had children of their own
Now when they look back on the fun that they had.

They understand why their mothers got mad
Now they can smile about the things that they did
And thank the guardian angels
They had when they were kids.
Dedicated to Mary Jane Stephens Hogg
December 15, 2002

Love to Bob

You're young once
And then the years add up
'Till they age you some
And you become eighty.

But you're still alert
And just as shiney
Smart enough to find my sister
For a while we thought you'd missed her.

As a brother-in-law
You've been great
Although you made the family wait
You're tried and true
And very clever
So I'd say, better late than never.
July 16, 2005

Craig and Rachel

Two little babies born in different states
Never met each other until a later date.
Two individuals growing as years passed
And in Florida—they finally met, at last.

The sweet tiny girl was a brown eyed beauty
A happy child that was loved –a plenty.
She liked to play dress-up and make believe
Her love for horses helped her to achieve.

She won many contests, getting blue ribbons
For her grace and skills in riding and jumping.
Now she is grown and has found her true love,
She's counting her blessings that come from above.

The baby boy was a joy to all who knew him
His golden blond hair, green eyes, and tan skin
Made for a handsome lad with a bright smile,
Was fun and could steal your heart all the while.

When he grew up, he was more than six feet tall
A charming man who was kind to one and all.
In South Carolina he has chosen his mate
He'll make her his wife and has named the date.

Wedding bells will ring on October 15, 2005
When Craig and Rachel become man and wife.
Friends and family will go to witness
Vows made to each other for marital bliss.

A Prayer for Craig and Rachel

Caring God, bless this pair
Remember to keep them in your care.
Always bless them through the years
Impede all danger, hurt, and tears.
Grant them wisdom to keep you near.

Always keep them close to you
Never forgetting your love so true.
Deepen their love for you—each other too.
Remain in their hearts, Lord
Always keeping your name adored
Holding on to all that is pure.
Envelop them in your loving arms
Lingering ever, keeping their marriage strong.

Dear Lord, I ask you to bless Craig and Rachel with a long, happy marriage, just as you have blessed me with mine. Amen.

Christina Colleen Cochran

Christina Colleen was a precious baby,
Born out west, where its cold and windy.
This pink bundle was a sunshine ray
Warming hearts on a bright spring day,
A blessing sent from Heaven on the fourth of May.

As Chrissy grew, she was of petite statue
With light brown hair and eyes of blue.
She was giggly and cute with a great big smile
Was pleasant and sweet and a happy child.
Could steal your heart in a very short while!

Chrissy's imagination was bigger than she,
She had a playmate that only she could see.
He seemed to be around when least expected.
Tony stayed hidden out and disconnected,
When something went wrong he was always suspected.

Chrissy grew out of her little girl things,
Thoughts turned to her guitar strings.
Soccer and school took up most of her time.
Knee problems from running proved unkind.
Changed plans for her future leaving soccer behind.

Chrissy graduated from West Florida University
Made her family proud with a business degree
She's a lovely young woman, all grown-up now.
Has fallen in love and ready to exchange her vows.
Congratulations, Mrs. Picheo. You may take a bow.
June 2006

Anthony Vito Picheo

Anthony Vito came on a September morn,
Making his parents proud of their fourth-born.
He was easy to care for and he seldom cried,
Was a handsome lad with clear blue eyes.

When asked what he played as a child,
He said, "Animals and books made me smile!"

His FFA and 4H clubs kept him occupied.
Time to play wasn't really justified.

Anthony did spend time at the fishing hole,
Catching bass and catfish made him happy, I was told.
When it came to reading, he chose non-fiction!
Make believe stuff doesn't keep his attention.

When asked about his favorites, he was quick to respond,
"Of Ford cars, western music, steak and potatoes, I am fond!"
Royal blue is his color and football his sport.
Florida University and the Gators he supports.

"Jaws" is his favorite movie and Chrissy is his girl.
He's as honest and true as a genuine pearl!
"Peach" is his nickname and a "sweet peach" is he,
A good man at heart for the whole world to see.
June 2006

A Prayer

As Anthony and Chrissy become man and wife, protect and guide them for the rest of their life, as one. Help them to always be true and love each other more and more each day. Please bless them with health, wealth, and happiness, and the time to enjoy all three.
Never let them forget that what they have or obtain comes from You. I pray that the happy times will for outweigh the hard ones. Give them strength to endure both the good and the bad.

Chrissy and Anthony

Chrissy and Anthony are a sweet couple to know.
Their love for each other always shows.
They met in Pensacola and fell in love.
They saw in each other a blessing from above.

Friends and family have come to see the wedding for Chrissy and Anthony.
In 2006 on the 15th of October, they will pledge their love to each other forever.
We wish them well for all the years to come, as they begin their new life together, as one.
June 2006

A Prayer for Chrissy and Anthony (Acrostic)

Christ, bless these two,
Hold them always close to you.
Reach into their loving hearts,
Increasing wisdom from the start
Strengthen their love through the years
Sharing and caring for each so dear
Your love can keep them, oh, so near.

Abate danger throughout their lives
Nurture them and help them thrive
Deepen their faith to help them survive.

Amplify your love and grace.
Nothing can ever take your place.
Together may they always be
Happy, loving, and worry free.

Only trust and respect for each,
Never forgetting their vows to keep.
Years will come and go with only good for them to reap.
June 2006
Dear Lord:
I ask you to bless Chrissy and Anthony with a long and happy marriage, just as you have blessed me with mine. Amen.

Dominic

Happy little Dominic
Laughs all the time
Except when he's hungry
And its time to dine.

His big eyes are twinkling
Blue as the sky
Except when he's sleeping
Or playing pee-pie.

Dominic is very smart
Quick as a flash
Walked, said Mama and Dada
Before his first year passed.

Dominic is a honey
Cute as he can be
To see him is to love him
A bundle of joy is he.
2009

2 On Holidays and Seasons

Autumn—A Month of Colors

Green, red, brown and yellow—leaves
Blue, azure, aquamarine, and indigo—skies
Silver, bronze, copper, and gold-fields
Black, white, and orange—Halloween.

October

October's such a pretty month
Leaves turn red, gold, and brown
They dance and spin,
Blow and fall,
And rustle to the ground.

October is an orange month
Pumpkins, moons, blazing trees
That shine and glow,
Sparkle and gleam,
With skies that warm and freeze.

October is a special month—
Harvest and Halloween
Ghosts, cats, goblins,
And crows in the corn.
Beautiful crops can be seen.

Fall Is Almost Here

Fall is almost here again
The weather is getting cooler

The nights are getting longer
And the days are getting shorter.

Fall is almost here again
The apples are ripe for picking
Pumpkins are big for carving
And the wood is cut for burning.

Fall is almost here again
Bringing bright cloudless skies of blue
Vivid colors of every hue
Scenes to paint—panoramic view.

Fall is almost here again
And it makes me very happy
It's good for my whole body
As it makes me smile a plenty.

Indiana in the Fall

Indiana in the fall—
What a sight to see!
Trees a-blaze
With orange, red, and gold!
A world of fantasies!

Indiana in the fall—
What bright skies of blue.
With birds flying south
A lovely autumn view!

Indiana in the fall—
Harvest time is here
Corn to reap

With crows in the field
Winter time is near!

Indiana in the fall—
A carpet on the ground—
Dance and swirl with falling leaves
A rustling taffeta sound!
1976

Halloween in Our Neighborhood

We live in a typical neighborhood
Where kids big and small trick-or treat
Some were dressed scary and some were very sweet
We had a bumble bee and several witches
Two came dressed in pirates breeches
One was a fairy and one was an angel
Both their wings looked very fragile
It is hard to describe all who came
They got popcorn and candy canes
Our welcome light was out by nine
We had served 48 by that time!

Halloween

All around the neighborhood
Ghosts and goblins travel
Door-to-door
Street-to-street
Scaring the people.

Old Turkey Gobbler

Old Turkey Gobbler in the barnyard sat,
Wondering if he should run or continue to sit.
He spread his tail feathers and started to strut,

Hoping to be thankful for some good luck.
Thanksgiving is coming and feasts are ahead!
Old Turkey Gobbler is saying his prayers!

Things to Be Thankful For

T enderness and mercy
H eavenly Father
A ll our blessings
N ice warm homes
K indness from others
S ons and daughters
G randchildren (7)
I illness free
V ery good children
I inventions that make life easier
N eeded medicines
G od's forgiveness

Thanksgiving

T hursday—the fourth one in November
H ome—where friends and family meet
A lways—counting our blessings
N ever-forgetting to thank God
K eeping—Thanksgiving in our hearts everyday
S sampling—all the good food.
G iving—a hand with the clean-up
I gnoring—our diets
V ery—happy to be together
I dentifying—our many blessings
N ever-forgetting the pumpkin pie
G athering—together to give thanks.
2009

Thanksgiving Prayer

I am thankful that Jesus died for me
For a life everlasting and that I'm free
To live my life without any fear
To speak, to read and choose what to hear
Also, I am thankful for my health
And able to have doctors to help me heal
With added blessings so many galore
My family, friends, home and much, much more.
2004

Preparing for Winter

Deep back in Stratford Hills
In an old sycamore tree
Lived a furry little family
As happy as can be
Three frisky ground squirrels—
Seymour, Shelton, and Shad.
All minded their mama, and pleased their dad.
Each worked hard to prepare for winter,
Gathering in fruits and nuts for future dinners.
Now their chores were completed,
It was time to party and work no more.
Many were invited to help celebrate.
Kin and neighbors, alike—
There were forty-eight.
Mama served corn cakes and walnut pies.
They ate so very much,
They all nearly died.
There were lots of games for the young to play,
Like acorn football and corn croquet.

The papas talked of seasons past,
While the mamas got to rest at last.

Finally a fiddler arrived to play some tunes.
They jigged and line danced, 'til way past noon.
When it finally came time to say, "Good night,"
All the welcomed guests scampered out of sight.
But before they left, they shook their bushy tails,
To say "thanks" politely, without fail.
And after the little family said their prayers,
They quickly climbed up the stairs.
Each snuggled down in their comfy beds,
And dreamed of frolicking in warm days ahead.
December 29, 2001

What is Christmas

Christmas is a time for giving and loving,
Giving of ourselves to help someone else,
Loving those who are needing someone's love,
Drawing nearer to our Heavenly Father.
Being thankful for all our blessings,
And showing our thankfulness in deeds of love and mercy
To me, this is CHRISTMAS.

Our Christmas Album

The pictures in this book
Have covered many a year
As you turn the pages to take a look
You have witnessed Christmas cheer.

The faces have expressed
Much love, joy, and laughter
Young and old with the Christmas spirit
Frozen then to view thereafter.

Decorations were displayed
In all their Christmas splendor
Some were simple and some were lavish
Depending on the facilitator.

It is fun to look back
At each year's celebration
Exalting Baby Jesus' birthday
Who provided our salvation.

2006 starts a new year
And this big book is bulging
So will close out the pages in this one
And begin a fresh new dawning.

Santa Is Love

To a little girl back in the 30's
Christmas was a long time coming
School was out for the holidays
But the days were long and dragging.

Her family gathered berries and cedar
To decorate the old farm house
Each child had hung up a stocking
Santa was all they could talk about.

Her Dad cut a tree to place in the hall
He nailed two boards to make a stand
Her Mama popped corn for a garland
With added ornaments—it looked grand!

The little girl snuck up to take a peek
Each day to check the Christmas tree
She'd go to see if Santa had come
In the night while she was asleep.

But one day, when she was doing her search
Nothing new was found on the tree
Then—she spied the guest bedroom door
She went in for a jumping spree.

The room was off limits—she knew quite well
For she had gone there before
To jump on the big old feather bed
Since she was there, she'd jump once more.

She took off her shoes and climbed up so high
Stood, jumped, and sprung in the air
She came down in a cloud—with a bang
Much to her surprise and despair!

So she carefully slide off the mountain
And peered under the spread to find
Many boxes there to keep
For Santa to render in time.

The little girl tugged at the biggest box
Until she could survey inside
The noise heard was a broken dish
She was big-eyed and mystified.

And with the box replaced, she left the room
And quickly went back down the hall
Eager to return the next day
To view all the contents in awe.

At first the forbidden trips were delightful
Each box held a new pleasure
Even the closet had surprises
Could Santa have left all the treasure?

The small fry left and started to wonder
Did Santa ever come early?
If so, why did we have to wait?
Why couldn't he spell correctly?

Why had Santa written, "Spiegel" for special?
On each and every brown box?
The same mark on a big book
That Mama kept under a lock.

The child was thinking about her discoveries
When she was trying to fall to sleep
Was there really a real Santa?
Couldn't he find their Christmas tree?

It suddenly dawned on her little brain
Not only was she misbehaving
But, she knew now for certain

There was no Santa—she began crying.

In the quiet of the night, her Mama came
Into her room and sat by her side
"Why are you crying, my little one?"
There was no use to denying.

With her arms thrown around her mother's neck
She poured out her confession
"And what's the worse," she exclaimed
"There is no Santa!" Was her conclusion.

Now the mama consoled her little girl
And gently wiped away her tears
"There is a Santa, if you believe
"Cause he is love and love is always near."

So now, when Christmas quickly rolls around
She remembers words spoken so dear
"There is a Santa, if you believe
"Cause Santa is love and love is always near!"
2004

Our Christmas Stockings

Our Christmas stockings were hung on the mantle
Nothing fancy or store bought
Mama's hosiery with runners
Were to hold what Santa brought.

When the long nylon stockings were filled
It could not hang by a nail
It's contents made it too heavy
Santa's generosity never failed.

Our names were written on a paper
And placed carefully in each sock
It really wouldn't have mattered
For each stocking got the very same lot.

There were oranges, apples, and bananas
Stuffed into the bulging cache
With nuts, candies, and sparklers
Making a very bountiful stash.

So when each stocking was filled with goodies
For each of us kid's delight
We savored each and every morsel
And kept our bounty out of sight.

It wasn't like we were all stingy
But, you see back then in those days
Treats were far and few in between
So the contents in each stocking was guarded and surveyed.

Valentine's Day

Valentine's Day is very special.
We select cards for different people.
Ones with love for moms and dads,
Ones with jokes for friends, we had.
Ones with lace for one true love.
Ones with hearts and turtle doves,
Secretly signing our names for none to see.
I'm hoping you'll have one for me.

A Favorite Day of Mine

Valentine's Day is a favorite day of mine.
That's when I get a lot of Valentines.
Big red hearts with lace and frills,
Asking, "Will you be my Valentine?"
And I answer quickly, "Yes, I will!"

A Valentine

I made you a Valentine!
Don't you think it's pretty?
With lace and ribbons
And bows so dainty
I made you a Valentine
'Cause I love you, Honey.

Valentine Candy

On Valentine's Day I get a lot of candy,
And I think that's really dandy!
Chocolate, red hots, and sugar hearts,
Mama makes cherry tarts
Sweet with sugar Valentine candy.
February 1982

A Valentine's Day Gift

A box of chocolate—
Flowers galore—
A ring for your finger,
From the one you adore.
A card with a message
With ribbon and lace,
Expressing the feelings
From the one you embrace.
2007

Cupid

Cupid shoots his arrow in the sky
Are any of us inoculated from his snare?
Run and hide, but no good does it do.
I fell in love, and so did you!
Nothing can prevent it when his arrow strikes
Go on and accept it without a fight!

What is a Valentine?

A Valentine is given to show that you care
It may be given to anyone or anywhere
It lets the person know just how you feel
The verse you choose must be real.

It may be light or of true devotion
Spend much time on your selection
Match each message with the person
So as to express the right emotion.

They're fun to get and fun to send
To one most dear, to friends and kin
Pick a card that's quick to say
What you want to acknowledge on Valentine's Day!

My Funny Valentine
(Bugs Bunny)

My funny little Valentine
I love your long pink ears
You make my heart beat so fast
I will surely faint, I fear!

My funny little Valentine
I love your big blue eyes
You make my head light with love
I'm cupid struck, I can't deny.

My funny little Valentine
I love your sunny smile
You make my life, Oh, so complete
You have knocked me off my furry feet!
That's love---folks!

My Valentine Toast

My toast goes to true love on Valentine's Day
I'm one of the lucky ones who can claim
A man that has been true to me
And me to him—the same!
Cheers!

My Favorite Valentine

My favorite Valentine is *you*, dear
It's been that way for years
Since I saw you first in fifty-one
In the contest of Valentines—you won.

My favorite Valentine is *you,* dear
You should know—never fear
Many, many years have come and gone
My love for *you* goes on and one.
Valentines Day--2009

V-A-L-E-N-T-I-N-E

V ery beautiful roses
A lot of ribbons and lace
L overs giving kisses
E ver loving wishes
N ever breaking promises
T ender love embraces
I nterludes and rendezvous
N ever broken vows
E xpression of love and caring.

Skunks

Do skunks send Valentines?
You bet they do!
They love each other
Just like me and you!

Looking Forward to Spring

I am looking forward to Spring
When the sun brings on the green
And flowers show their faces
Creating a very colorful scene.

I am looking forward to Spring
When the warm days are longer
Time spent outside is welcome
To observe God's beauty and splendor.

I am looking forward to Spring
Happy to tell winter good-bye
Packing all my winter clothes away
Staying warm with the sunny skies.
2009

March Wind

Winds are howling, winds are blowing
Bringing in lots of snow
Winds are gusting, winds are bending
All the trees and plants below.

March

March what are you?---Lion or Lamb?
Are you kind? Are you wild?
Will you blow strong or mild?
Which one will you decide to be?
Let the sun shine and favor me!

March 25, 1993

Not a sky in the clouds
It all seems so gray
I'm praying to God
Larry's problems will go away
I must be brave
And look through the clouds
With faith I'll see
A blue sky without fail.

Tulip Time

Tulip time is coming!
I can hardly wait—
To see the beautiful colors
Please, don't be late.

Tulip time is coming!
Spring is almost here.
Little tulips nodding—

Standing tall to cheer.
Tulip time is coming
My favorite time of the year.

A Pretty Irish Poem

I am Irish and for that I am proud
Three cheers for the Irish
I shout out loud
Sur'in Tom Smith was Grandpa's name
It is said his mother from Ireland came
A beautiful auburn was her hair
And eyes so green that people stared
A bit of me grandmother, my Mama would say
Was born in me in March one day.

Eating Our Greens

When it's dinner time—
We Irish think green
Green is the color of our beans.
We always want green apple pie,
And a big leafy salad on the side.

If it's tea, we always have green!
We sprinkle parsley on nearly everything
Green peppers are especially good.
And a meal without pickles—
We never would.

We love our greens—Three times a day.
Even green eggs in the early morn.
Will bring a smile to the most forlorn.
So don't deny us our delicious greens
Or a temper tantrum is sure to be seen!

If I Catch A Leprechaun

I have often been told
If I catch a leprechaun
He'll give me gold.
If I'm lucky
And he gives gold to me
I'll thank him quickly
And set him free.
I'll spend my gold wisely
And not waste a bit!
I'll save for the future
And not lose my wits!
Mind you, it's easier to spend
Than it is to save
But remember, my friend
You can't take it to the grave.
So, I'll spend enough to enjoy my life
And refrain from hording without any strife.
It's March and I'm looking for a leprechaun
If I catch one, it'll be a *real* phenomenon.

A Ring of Mushrooms

A ring of mushrooms around a tree,
Just appeared over night for us to see.
Was it little fairies that put them there?
Did they hold a meeting last night,
If so, what did they declare?
Was it good luck to each who stopped to wonder?
Many passed, never pausing to let their minds ponder.

A ring of mushrooms circled a tree,
Who placed it there has puzzled me.
Was it leprechauns who did all the work,
In the moonlight on the lawn after dark?
If so, what brought on the perk?
It wasn't there yesterday, I know for sure,
Because I looked at the very spot
Where the tree was secured.

A ring of mushrooms surrounded a tree,
How it got there just baffles me?
Perhaps green frogs put them in formation
And sat on them while they gave their attention
To voting on all of the important equations.
Regardless of who, why or the reason,
I'm still astonished at the curious sight,
Of the ring of mushrooms that appeared over night!

Another Birthday

March has brought another birthday
It's hard for me to believe
Fifty nine years have come and gone
But life's been good to me!
March 1993

Birthday #75

I turned seventy-five today.
I can't believe it!
It seems like just yesterday
I was only twenty.

I am thankful for all my years
God's been good to me!
He has blessed me many ways—
Health, friends, family, and parents so dear!
March 12, 2008

A Leprechaun Lyric

Little leprechaun, wearing green
Coming out to be seen
On St. Paddy's Day down in the glen
Dancing in the shamrocks
Singing your songs
Bringing your laughter all day long
Stay a little longer, don't go away!
Why do you come for just one day?

An Easter Acrostic

E is for an *ever* loving Father who gave his only son
A is for *always* forgiving the wrongs we've done
S is for our *Savior* who died for our sins
T is for our Heavenly *trip* we'll take at the end
E is for *entering* Paradise, if we've loved the Lord
R is for the *rest* we'll find in the arms of God.

The Earth Is Happy

The earth is happy today
For new life has begun.
God sent his only son
So that we might live on.
Jesus died on the cross

To take our sins away.
He arose from the grave
So we can do the same.
The earth is happy today.
Easter 2009

Easter Baskets

Easter baskets filled with bright colored eggs
Brought by the bunny with graceful legs
He leaves candy and surprises for little ones
Hopping along as he merrily goes
Wiggling his ears and winkling his nose.

3 On Events and Locations

A Good—Bye to Indiana

Good—bye to Indiana
I hate, but I need to go.
I have mixed emotions—You can tell, I know!
I will miss your cornfields—green and cream.
I'll miss your trees ablaze—a beautiful scene.
I'll miss your sweet aroma—of honeysuckle vine.
I'll miss the pink sunsets at twilight time.
I'll miss the basketball games—and the scores.
Now that I have started—I could list a lot more.
I'll miss my big house—on Avalon Drive,
And the cozy dinners—by the fireside.
Mostly I'll miss my friends—young and old.
But I'll not miss your winter—icy cold.
Good—bye Indiana.
1998

San Antonio

San Antonio is a beautiful city,
Nestled in its rolling hills.
A golden city of sunshine—
At nights sparkling lights that thrill.

San Antonio is an exciting city
With Fiesta Texas, River Walk,
Sea World, Breckenridge Park,
And sport arenas that "Spurs" the talk.

San Antonio is a historical city,
Especially around 1835
Bowie, Houston, and Crockett
Fought to keep Texas alive.

San Antonio is a romantic city,
For there—it's easy to love.
The music and splashing colors
And the sound of the turtle doves.

San Antonio is a military city,
Randolph, Kelly, Lackland, Brooks
And the old Sam Houston Fort
Bring many to the city, who never depart.

And we can't forget the Alamo,
Bluebonnets, poinsettias, and oaks
Round cacti and lazy mesquites
They all make up San Antonio,
A city—that can't be beat!
2008

A Trip to San Antonio

To San Antonio town—returning
Dan will be there to meet us.
If we ever leave St. Louis
Hurry pilot—can't you see
It's southern bound I want to be.

Twenty-five more minutes
I can't believe it
The flight attendant just assured us
All flights are running late

She's return to inform us—our gate.

Flying in circles makes me antsy
I hope the tank is full—not empty
Larry is getting restless, too

We could have driven—but we flew
It will be worth it though—I'm sure
If we are able to endure.

24,000 feet up in the sky
In a circle we are cruising
How many times must we go around
Waiting our turn for a landing
Over San Antonio we are hovering
People laughing, people talking
I'm anxious and I'm yearning.
We finally arrive at gate 24
Dan was waiting at the airport door.
We greeted him with loving arms
So happy to be in the South once more.

The Traffic Outside Our Windows

The traffic outside our window
Isn't the usual kind.
There are no horns blowing,
No tickets issued for speeding.
It's traffic of a different kind.

As we watch through the window,
We are often quite amazed,
At sights that we behold.
A squirrel may be seen flying

To the feeder sending birds in a craze.

Suddenly there's a traffic jam,
Everyone is trying to land.
The space is way too small,
Causing bumps and bangs and some falls
To the ground creating soft feather fans.

Our eyes see all kinds of action:
Swift, darting, jumping, motion
Zipping, zooming, dashing,
Sprinting, scooting, hopping, so fast
Each one seeking a safe destination.

Not all the traffic is swift!
Some are unusually slow,
Like worms, snails and turtles
Caterpillars, slugs, and some frogs.
Their movements: to and fro or stop and go.

Some traffic just flutters and flit,
Like from flower to flower,
Not sure which way to go.
All have a reason to travel,
Wasps, bumble bees, butterflies, cruise for hours.

Two modes of travel cause skirmish
When a snake or mouse appears
We, then are motivated
And the inside traffic takes over,
We're out the door and soon the highway is clear.

The traffic parades with color
All hues and tints are present

Reds, yellows, greens, and blues
Gold, silver, white, gray, black and brown.
Pausing to see the show is time well-spent.

The traffic supplies amusement.
The acts are entertaining.
Some selfish, like people,
Some helpful and very caring.
Some antics are beyond our explaining.

It's a gift to watch the traffic
Outside our big window pane!
We can view God's creatures
Which are unaware of our stares,
Where we're awed again, again, and again!
August 2010

A Tampa Sunset

What a breathtaking sunset, for eyes to behold.
Captured with a camera, pink, red, and gold.
What a radiant sunset, witnessed by three
Frozen on paper, for you to see.
What a Florida sunset, with glorious hues,
Apprehended on film, treasured to view.
What a moment together—we'll never forget.
We paused to absorb, God's marvelous sunset.
January 2008

A Rainbow in Destin

I just saw a rainbow,
It took my breath away!
God unfurled his banner
His colors to display.
Who could doubt, not I.
Each color is a promise
Written clear across the sky.

With green he reminded us
To have faith and believe.
His son redeemed our sins
And he saved you and me.
He died on a cross
And the third day he arose,
So, we can be saved-not-lost.

Yellow reflects beauty
God made in each of us,
To help identify
Our talents and thus--
Know how to serve Him
While we are down here on earth.
We're his children, his heavenly gems.

Blue recalls our blessings
So many from above.
Don't forget to count them
The biggest one is love.
Look hard to see them
Sometimes blessings are disguised,
Only realized when time has passed by.

Orange stands for compassion

Something everyone needs.
A love for each other
A caring heart is free.
Stand in their shoes,
Help share their sorrow and pain,
God's work can be done through you.

Lavender means kindness
It doubles in return.
A color—hard to see
Look closely—it's lovely.
God's specialty
Think of others before yourself
Kindness can be done so easily.

Red shades are important
Telling us all to pray
Late in the evening
Or any time of day.
God always hears.
Look at the rainbow and you will know
That God is always near.
1998

Down by the Seaside

Under a big umbrella—down by the sea,
Taking it easy—nothing bothering me.
Watching the waves crashing so free,
Rolling and curling clear—then white as can be.

All around me is sunshine warming the sand.
Here I sit with a book in my hand,
Relaxing and thinking how lucky I am
Down by the seaside with my favorite man!

A sandpiper and seagull stand waiting to see,
If their dinner will come in with the sea.
A little crab runs sideways to hide,
Back to its hole to escape passers by.

Couples in swim wear stroll hand-in-hand,
Leaving their footprints in the sand.
Waves come in one by one erasing their patterns,
Rolling forever never ceasing to come.

Over the roar of the surf—voices can be heard.
Small children are laughing and chasing the birds.
They have tired of sandcastles—refusing to stand.
Mothers smear sunscreen to prevent a tan.

My eyes leave my book—what do I see?
A sailboat, sailing so leisurely
Out on the emerald water with sand so white.
Down by the seaside—a spectacular sight!
August 2001

Oh! To See a Texas Sky

Oh! To see a Texas sky
Is to see a great blue wonder,
There is no limit for your eye
A vast kaleidoscope to ponder.

Oh! To see a Texas sky
Is to me the greatest pleasure.
I can truly answer you why
Its beauty cannot be measured.

Oh! To see a Texas sky
With a million stars to picture

And an immense moon hanging high,
A beautiful sight to capture.

Oh! To see a Texas sky
Is to see the widest jumbo,
Stretching and hovering high
From Texarkana to El Paso.

Oh! To see a Texas sky
Is to see a magnificent sight,
If you've experienced it, like I—
Seen from the ground or from a flight.

Oh! To see a Texas sky
It simply takes you breath away
With an umbrella rainbow so high,
An arch of colors on display.

Oh! To see a Texas sky
It will be my last endeavor,
To be buried when I die
Under the gigantic Texas sky.
May 2005

Katrina

On August 28, 2005 Katrina roared in with all her fury,
She ripped and tore relentlessly causing much misery,
Seeing the havoc this vixen created is hard to possibly envision,
With speed and force she generated horror and complete confusion.

This ugly, cruel bisector vowed to do her very "best" *worst,*
While swirling and building out over the water—to hate and anger she gave birth.
Determined to be remembered for most evil deeds that no storm had done before.
So eagerly she began cutting, crushing, and crumbling as soon as she reached shore.

Broken parts, pieces, and people were flying—crashing from the wind,
Baffled minds and tortured bodies were scathed by Katrina again and again.
Destruction all around them so quickly in disarray—sights too ugly to comprehend,
The violent boorish actions of the uninvited guest was pure hell at her command.

Just when darkness and calm began to render in the tattered ravaged land,
Katrina caught her breath and quickly looked down to check her skills firsthand,
Before she departed, she wanted to make sure she'd always be remembered,
So she blew and spat more rain 'till Lake Pontchartrain could no longer be contained.

The calling card she left behind was pitiless and engulfing with chaos, death, and drownings,
Deluge from mud, heat, decay, waste, and stench was putrid and choking.
Things that once were present will never again be there or the same,
Katrina definitely made certain she gained the highest nobility and prestigious fame.

But out of all this spoil and suffering God's love never fails,
Many who had less than nothing now have hope to prevail.
Katrina's maliciousness will always be remembered and her strength marveled by all,
But so will the kindness of God's people whose generosity has appalled.
September 2005

Rita

Rita and Katrina made quite a pair
Both of their visits left nothing, but despair.
Twin sisters with destruction on their minds
These wind witches were everything, but kind.

Churning in the Gulf, Rita took her time
Keeping us guessing, this partner in crime.
To compound suffering was her main goal
She wanted everything "out of control."

Rita wobbled and bobbled diverting her track
Causing two million to leave in a pack.
At the last minute, she quickly turned east
Showing herself as a terrible beast.

Her arrival was a double whammy
With devastation and catastrophe.
Everything in Rita's, path was destroyed
She made everyone's life hectic and void.

After demolishing all that she could
Rita surveyed towns that were piles of wood.
Her finale was never faltered
She left land completely slaughtered.

Leaving many homeless and powerless
Rita was happy, and left a big mess.
Now it is up to the ones that were spared
To help the forlorn, and show how they care.

Rita has passed on now and everyone's glad
Her ruination has left so many sad.
This season for hurricanes is almost gone
It is hoped we'll never host another one.
October 2005

Ike

Ike, the big brother of Katrina and Rita,
Wanted to top their reputations.
He had the whole world watching,
As he prepared to create his destruction.

Brawny Ike left Cuba in absolute shambles,
Then entered the Gulf for a breather.
Flexing his muscles to rest,
To dream and scheme up his worst displeasures.

Ike embodied the complete mass of water,
In slow motion while he pondered.
How he could cause the most damage,
Reeking havoc, devastation, and squander.

Big Ike created a zone of uncertainty,
With his giggling, wobbling, bobbling,
To keep everyone guessing,
While gaining massive strength for subduing.

Cruel Ike's big eye was the largest cavity,
Any hurricane had ever had.
He eyed in on Bolivar,
Selecting a sight for his launching pad.

Ike's aim was to take the complete coast of Texas,
Then move on to broaden his field,
With ruin, rack, chaos, and pain,
Claiming "King of Destruction" on his shield.

Ike was hovering off the coastline with darkness,

Gaining in power and energy,
Clashing—splashing brown water,
Sending in sludge and nasty debris.

Lucifer Ike was enjoying the attention,
While people were glued to the TV's,
Watching to heed precautions,
Hoping to ward off the devil's destiny.

Many foolish people told Ike "to take a hike,"
Failing to take him seriously,
Sad to say on the next day,
With regret—surrendered to misery.

Enormous Ike's voice roared in *loud* fortissimo!
Making it known to all he was here.
Not leaving 'til he was sure,
He'd be long remembered after he disappeared.

Blowing, bending, crushing, rolling, ripping, tearing, trashing,
Ike accomplish these with all his strength,
Drowning, drenching---exploding!
Mandating horror throughout his journey's length.

Ruthless Ike left a trail of shock and disbelief,
Tossing cars and boats like little playthings,
Leaving piles of pick-up-sticks,
Changing lives forever with his brutal fling.

Monstrous Ike caused island towns to lose their grip,
Swift, deep, surge swept them far out to sea.
Leaving beaches ravished,
The beauty wrecked by his selfish deed.

Texas couldn't satisfy his wicked violation.
He had set his sinful goals very high,
To beat his siblings' records.
He moved northeast to cause more hell before he died.

Actually, it's a "toss up" to see who did the worst!
Was it Katrina, Rita, or Ike?
It depends on the victims,
To grade the hurricanes that dealt each strike.

They all three were successful in robbing necessities,
Leaving a lot of people in need,
Ending many styles of life,
Filling their own greed by relentless speed.

Many hurricanes have come with fury and wrath,
But after each horrendous act,
Their meanness produced kindness,
As God's people help each other to come back.
September 2008

Class of 1950

Pony tails and crew hair cuts
Poodle skirts and bobby socks
Loafers and saddle oxfords
Rock-n-roll and teeny boppers.
We were so young—
Do you recall, what went on in Temple halls?
We can laugh now when we compare
How simple things were then and there,
But we were so eager—
Our futures to begin.
Fifty years have come and gone

Hard to believe how time has flown.

College years and wedding bells
And for some visa-versa
Don't we wish we had known then
What all the years have taught us.
Our first apartments, bigger cars, growing families
Traveling to places near and far.
Good times and bad times—
We've laughed and cried through many.
Now my friends, as we sit here—
Thinking and reminiscing,
The fact we're here is quite a blessing!

Traditions and Temple High
Still live in our hearts.
The spirit of Wildcats
We've had from the start.
We have found "a silver lining"
In our golden years.
Wave high our class colors, green and white, we cheer
The rose was our flower, our teachers were the best
The class of 1950 stood out above the rest!
So friends raise your glasses, a toast to each and everyone
Celebrate 2000—fifty years have come and gone.
May 5, 2000

Another Class Reunion

Five more years have come and gone!
Can you believe it?
Seems like only yesterday—
We celebrated our fiftieth
When we came together to recall

Good ole days in Temple High halls.

In spite of many years,
We still remember
Our class of nineteen-fifty,
When we were so young and skinny
Let's raise our glasses and give three cheers
In homage of our senior year.

Regardless of our aches and pains
Gray hair and the such
We may have slowed down a bit
But we know we're a lucky bunch
To be so fortunate to proclaim
The class of "1950" and its fame.

Our colors were chosen well
Salute: green and white
Our flower—we picked the rose
To show composure and repose
Our motto had a lesson to tell
"Life is a picture, paint it well!"

Sing of the "silver lining"
A song close at heart
We've kept the wildcat spirit
That we've all had from the start
It's sustained us to our golden years
And it will, till we depart.

Let's pause to reminisce
All the years gone by,
We're too young to be so old
But our true age we can't deny.

We may rock and roll with Medicare—
But the class of "1950" is still debonair!

If anyone should happen to ask
We can tell them why.
The class of nineteen fifty
Was outstanding at Temple High.
We worked hard, played hard, and did our best
Never shirking a single quest.

Now we're here in 2005
Thanks to Lipitor and Celebrex,
We're able to run and play—
Cherishing the good old days.
So whoop it up, "Class of 1950"
We've still got our "get-up-and-go"
We may be a little slower, but
Try not to let it show.
January 25, 2005

Class Reunion In 2008

Class of 1950—we meet again.
Isn't it great to see old friends.
What a lucky bunch we are
To have lived so long and come so far!

To the Class of '50—I'd say like to say
I'm proud of you in every way
I'm thankful that I'm one of you
To Temple High we've all been true.

Fifty-eight years have passed—how could it be?
Why did time pass so hurriedly?

Our busy lives made us unaware
'Til we stop, like now, counting to compare

We were seniors then, and we're seniors now.
We rocked then, and we rock now.
Our pony tails and crew cuts may have grayed,
But our Temple High spirit has never strayed.

Our motto—"Life is a picture—paint it well,"
Our colors—green and white—still prevails,
Our flower—the beautiful rose,
Our song—"Look for a Silver Lining"—
Still in our hearts a sweet repose.

So the class of 1950, as we celebrate—
Remember it's great to reach 2008
Let's count our blessings, one by one
Thanking God for all he's done.
'Til our next time together—here's to everyone.
May 2008

Reunion in 2010

Well, it's two thousand and ten!
How lucky can we be?
That the class of 1950
Is quite blessed, we all agree!

Sixty years have come and gone
It is hard to believe!
So long ago and yet it seems
Like yesterday we took our leave!

We were so young and eager
To exit Temple High
Not taking time to savor youth
Ready to spread our wings and fly.

Our steps were fast and steady
Ready to start a new escapade
With a diploma in our hands
Assured we had made the grade.

With the "Wildcat Spirit" in us
We faced our daily chores
And worked to achieve our goals
Like we were instructed before.

Our class was optimistic
In the class song we choose
Oh! Look for the Silver Lining
Kept us calm when problems arose.

Our motto—*Life's a picture*—
And we've painted it well
So members of our senior class
Here's to us—we still excel.

Our flower was the lovely rose
Another choice we made
Proved our Class of '50 had class
The Class with class, is still portrayed.

Green and white were our colors
Green means to go—don't stop
We were way ahead of our time
Today—Green is at the top.

This reunion is oh, so special
To greet each of our friends
To count our many blessings
Too many to comprehend.

As members of the '50 Class
Our hearts swell with pride
The start we got at Temple High
Was the best, we can't deny.

So here's to the Class of 1950
May the memories of our past
Be held deep within our hearts
For we know the good times we had together
Will never be surpassed.
2010

4 On Animals and Humor

Ischa

Ischa, is my kitty cat
Wherever I am, that's where she's at
She likes to sit upon my lap
She minds the house when I nap.

Ischa, is a pretty cat
White and fluffy and so soft to pet
Her graceful paws are streaked with gray
Like she walked through dirt coming my way.

Ischa, is an intelligent cat
Knows when it's time to eat and things like that
She's very happy and purrs a lot
She'll always love me and forgets me not.

Ischa, is a green-eyed cat
The friendliest cat you ever met
I love her and she loves me
That is plain for all to see.
Written for Zetta DeVoe
March 2006

Roo, My Pony

Roo, my little painted pony
Is a princess, I know,
Because when she eats her oats
She holds one hoof just so!

I love my little pony, Roo
I ride her when I can
She greets me with a kiss
When I hold out my hand.

Roo is such a pretty pony
Her colors are outstanding
With shades of brown and black
On a canvas of white surrounding.

Roo doesn't like apples
I found this out quite fast
I gave her some—she took a bite
And she quickly spat it back.

If you ever see my pony—
I know you will agree,
She's the cutest little filly,
That you'd ever hope to see.

I'll always love my Roo
And she'll always love me
She's very sweet and gentle
She makes me happy as can be!
March 12, 2008

My Little Me Me

My rambunctious little Me Me
You've stolen my heart away.
You scurry here and you scurry there
Bouncing with happy play.

My own bright-eyed little Me Me
A gray and white powder puff
Black lines accentuates your beauty
You are so soft to touch.

My intriguing little Me Me
You really are quite a tease.
You have never ceased to amaze me
Always doing as you please.

My ever loving little Me Me
You're so very dear to me.
You kept me from being bored or lonely.
I love your company.

I'm very, very grateful, Me Me
To my friends who gave me, *you*
For you are truly a treasure
And to them I say, *Mew, Mew!*
2007

What Kind of Shoes

An Indian wears moccasins
A cowboy wears boots
An islander wears sandals
Or goes without shoes.

A swimmer wears flippers
An athlete wears cleats
A dancer wears tap shoes
Or ballet for the feet.

A baby wears booties

A papa wears spats
A mama house shoes
Or something like that.

A fireman wears galoshes
A China man wears thongs
A princess wears slippers
That aren't very long.

An Eskimo wears snowshoes
A skier wears skis
A skater wears ice skates
Or roller or blades.

A model wears high heels
A golfer—golf shoes
When a person is lazy
It's loafers—he'll choose.

A tennis player wears sneakers
A teenager wears clogs
A fisherman wears hip boots
When down in the bogs.

A sick person wears bed shoes
To keep the feet warm
A farmer wears rubbers
When down on the farm.

An astronaut wears moon shoes
A runner wears spikes
A soldier in combat
Wears boots to fight.

A horse wears horseshoes
A kitten wears none
A horse has work to do
A kitten has fun!

There are beach and water shoes
All made of mesh
Addias and Nikes
That made quite a flash!
A doctor wears cloth shoes
Sterilized for sanitation
To operate and articulate
For surgical perfection.

So many to choose from
A purpose to fill
The brand, style, and color
Command as you will.

Remember to choose comfort
Support and size
Be good to you tootsies
It's smart and so wise!
January 1995

Witchita

Which witch is which
It's hard to tell
Made from a wine bottle
Witchcraft is her spell.

Her head is round
Her eyes are coal
Her hair is black and straight
She'll never grow old.

Her nose is sharp
Made from a knife
Her broom made of pine needles
Give her speed in flight.

A spider on hat
A ring to match
With long pointed fingers
To stir and scratch.

A pot full of brew
With frogs and lice
Lizards and dragonflies
Makes it twice as nice.

Her creation
Was not to scare
Was to save the bottle
When the wine's no longer there
Cheers to Witchita the witch!
October 2008

Silly Willy and Loosey Goosey

Silly Willy said, "Oh! Fiddle-faddle!
I'll not be a fuddy-duddy—I'll eat a tutti-frutti!"

"Don't be a lony-tuney!" said a sassy lassie.
"You sound wishy-washy—is your brain topsy-turvy?
Do you want to be roly-poly or itty-bitty?"

"You are such a Loosey Goosey—stop that jibber-jabber.
Look in your savy-baggy and get some jingle-jangle.
Forget the nitty-gritty—it's not hari-kari.
I'm sure it will be hunky-dory to spend a teensy-weensy.
On some yummy-gummy, if you don't tittle-tattle!"

"Okie-dookie, lovely-dovey, you know I'm your tootsie-wootsie.
I'll stop the chitter-chatter—I won't dilly-dally.
I'll hippity-hoppity and pitter-patter, not widdle-waddle to the store!
You dipzy-doodle, there'll be no hanky-panky,
Or you will see your honey-bunny ziggle-wiggle never more!"
April 2000

Where Is It?

Is it up or down,
Is it gone or around?
Is it in or out,
Is it here or about?

It is under or over,
Is it seen or undercover?
Is it above or below,

Where it is, I do not know?

Is it backward or forward,
Is it inside or outward?
Is it here or there,
Is it anywhere?

Is it absent or present,
Perhaps it could be transparent?
Is it before or beyond,
Is it concealed or in the open?

Is it north, south, east or west,
Where it is I cannot guess?
Is it invisible or plain to see,
Is it lost for eternity?

Is it near or is it far,
Is it in the house or the yard?
Is it behind or in front
Is it hidden in a trunk?

Is it in heaven or is it in hell,
Where it is, I cannot tell?
I have looked, looked, and looked,
Will you help me find my book?
October 2003

Arthritis

Arthritis is his real name.
I call him Arthur for short.
He is a guest, I don't welcome.
I've not liked him from the start!

He comes when least expected.
I can't recall his first visit.
It wasn't in my younger years.
Arthur's call—I'd never forget it!

I'd ask him to schdoodle,
It wouldn't do any good!
He comes and goes on his own time.
I'd send him packing if I could!

He's a real pain in the neck.
Zaps you here and zaps you there,
There's no telling where he'll strike next!
His routine visits don't seem fair!

There's no exact time, day or night,
Arthur may come a-calling.
He has a schedule of his own!
Your time, he's always demanding!

When Arthur extends his stay,
And it is more than I can bear,
Many remedies I depend on—
Ointments, heat, pills, and an easy chair!

Arthur may drop or pop in.
Always there when it's raining.
Causing my joints to ache and throb!
He's always poking and jabbing!

Arthur is always looking,
To cause as much pain as he can.
He has no favorite victim,

But sometimes, I think that I am!

Arthur has lived forever,
Much to everyone's sorrow.
Mama knew him—Grandpa knew him,
Arthur's travel plans are confirmed for all tomorrow!
November 1, 2009

What We Planned to Do, But Didn't on Labor Day

Do the yard and mow the grass.
Wash the windows and shine the glass.
Clean the house and do the clothes.
Wash the car with the garden hose.
Paint the roof and pay the rent.
Hoe the garden and mend the fence.
All these things we meant to do
But instead we labored not
Our excuse is *we forgot!*
1983

Things Not To Be Afraid Of!

A barking Ben
A little lamb
A sleeping lion
A dead fly
A loving mom
Things you don't know about
An old pumpkin carved
A candy wrapped.

Double "OO"s

A ghost says "Boo!"
An owl says "Whoo!"
The wind says "Woo!"
For a fly it's "Shoo!"
A pigeon says "Coo!"
A cow says "Moo!"
Many animals in a "zoo!"
A train goes "Choo-choo!"
A rooster—"cock-a-doodle-doo!"
It's sticky with "goo!"
My hair needs "shampoo!"
An Eskimo's home—"igloo!"
My pony's name is "Roo!"
Me? I love you, "too!"
A child cries "Boo-hoo!"
When he gets a "boo-boo!"
A sneeze us a "ah-choo!"
A baby says "Goo-goo!"
The tree is a "bam-boo!"
I've got to stop—
I think I'm going "coo-koo!"
2011

A Gal Named Zetta

Zetta—is such a pretty name!
Do you mind—if I ask
Just how you got it?
"Of course, I don't mind,"
Was the reply
"Not even a little bit!"
"You see," she said, "when I was born
Daddy asked my mother

To name me Zetta
For an old girlfriend
Who had been so kind
That he couldn't forget her."

My mother granted my father's wish
Cunningly adding Vonciel
For he was the man
She also said "yes" to
Before meeting and giving
My father her hand.

Now Zetta Vonciel confided
That she's only met two others
In all her lifetime
With the same name as Zetta.
Was the girlfriend so kind
That two others couldn't forget her?
Written for Zetta Vonciel Jaye DeVoe
February 2006

5. On Reflection

I Am Thankful

I am thankful that Jesus died for me
For the life everlasting and that I am free
To live my life without any fear
To listen, to speak, and choose what to hear
Also, I'm thankful for my health
And able to have doctors to help me heal
With added blessings so many galore
My family, friends, home and much, much more.
2005

The Food of Love

What is your favorite?
So many to choose from!
There are sugar cookies, candies
And cakes made with rum.
There are gooey brownies
Or pancakes stacked high
With sweet flavored syrups—
Or strawberry pie.

You may choose macaroons,
Caramels, custards or ice cream.
Which morsel will please you
With sugar supreme?
They all must have sugar
Oh! Sugar, so sweet!
'Cause that's what makes
"The Food of Love," so complete.

Sing Out America

Sing out America
Sing in harmony
Tell the world we're united
Never divided will be.

Sing out America
Raise your voices loud
Tell all the world we're free
And of that we are so proud.

Sing out America
Sing of hope and care
Tell all the world we stand together
With the grace of God through prayer.

Sing out America
At this time of despair
Inform all our enemies
Their evil deed we now share.

Sing out America
Make the notes prevail
We stand and fight together
We'll not falter, fall, or fail.

Sing out America
Sing with broken hearts
But our country will grow stronger
Our victory toll impart.
After 9/11

Happy Birthday America

It is our country's birthday
Hooray for the red, white, and blue
Wave old glory proudly
It stands for freedom for me and you!

It is our country's birthday
Two hundred and nineteen years
We all love our America
For her we stand and cheer.

What Love Is

Love is heavenly to many people and hell to some.
Some lovers play for keeps, and some for fun.
Love is meant to be tender, caring and kind,
Forever forgiving, understanding, sublime,
Full of loyalty, truthfulness, and devotion
With acts of romance, pleasure, and passion.
I'm an example of one who knows the true meaning
I've been bountifully blessed with love, sustaining
By family, friends, and most of all by God.
2011

The Good Life

When you're too old to work
And too young to die
God blesses you with time to live
The good life—not to be denied.

Be careful not to waste it
You're a chosen few

Not everyone is so lucky
Each day has a beautiful hue.

Try to savor each moment
Don't forget to pray
Be thankful for the time you have
To recall the good old days!
2006

Pictures

Pictures permit us to recall
Moments frozen for us all
Never again will that time be
Memories captured for us to see.

Keep you camera close at hand
Snap a photo if you can
It will be treasured—I am sure
Fleeting glances of time secured.

Where Have All the Years Gone?

Where have all the years gone?
I often ask myself
Perhaps, I fell asleep,
And didn't see them pass.
I remember playing dolls
And dressing up my cats.
I remember my first high heels
And trivial things like that,
But why can't I recall just how
The time passed so fast?
Could it be I blinked my eyes

And I forgot to ask
The time of day when I was small
And waited an eternity for Christmas to come at last!

Where have all the years gone?
I often ask myself
How could it be that yesterday
I watched our children play
And kissed them each
Unaware that time mysteriously cheats.
Decades came and decades went
In blocks of time and space
Mirrors reflect the fleeting time
By lines on my inquiring face!

Where have all the years gone?
Could it possibly be
I failed to look at the calendar
And the pages flew so free.
Now we have our grandchildren
In their teens, when it seems
Like yesterday we bounced them our knees.

Now that it is time to retire
I ask myself
Where have all the years gone
And will life slow down
Or go just as fast
As Mother said it would?
The older you get the faster time flies
And no one seems to know the reason why?

Where have all the years gone?
I guess I'll just have to say

Each precious moment slipped away
Day after day after day!
1990

Relaxing After Work

It's nice after a day's work
To come home and crash
Whether it's with tea, soda,
Or a cocktail in a glass.
It seems to help end the day!
It feels good when you get home
To prop your feet up high
Let your mind become idle
Leaving your labor behind.

Some people don't relax after work
They commit their all to their job.
They cheat themselves and loved ones, too
Of the joys that work often robs.
2011

America

From the North, to the South
To the East, to the West
America is a beautiful sight to behold
With her orchards and grain fields,
Her rivers and mountains
And buildings small and bold.
America I love you
With freedom for us all.

Beautiful Things

Lovers holding hands
Castles in the sand
Bright red tulips in a row

Footprints pressed upon the snow
Red hearts with ribbons,
Edged with lace.
Hugs and kisses to embrace
A whisper of "I love you."
Beautiful things—here's just a few.

Green Things

Green frogs
Green thumbs
Green beans
Green apples
Green grapes
Pickles
Turtles
Grass
Bees
Peas
Snakes
Envy
Green as a gourd
Fern, moss, chlorophyll
Irish bells upon a hill.

Food—Thoughts of Love

Chocolate kisses
Angel food cake
Heart shaped cookies
An Alaskan baked
Boxes of candy
Roses and wine
Two lips forever
Will you be mine?

Gestures of Romance

Holding hands
Taking walks
Hugs and kisses
Whispering secrets
Love letters
Golden rings
Bouquets of flowers
Talking for hours
Chocolate candy
Wine and roses
Lovers forever
Romantic music
Slow dancing

1950 Memories of Temple High

Come go with me down memory lane
Back to our high school years.
Remember our good and gentle life
So distant yet so near.

One memory can bring to mind another
Help me and we'll recall.
The good times that we had together
There was fun for us all.

Every Friday night after games
We danced the night away.
The boys twirled girls around the floor.
What memories—need I say!

Some strolled down the halls hand-in-hand.
Some known to steal a kiss.
To most of us it was puppy love,
A few found wedded bliss.

Looking back some of you will recall
Some pranks not fun for all.
Details can only be told by few
Simple words create the view.

Football pants, fire drills, peanut butter,
Or penny-ante poker,
I'll name no names, so please don't ask me
Who was the funny joker?

Our coaches worked us extremely hard

To help us win our games.
Hilley's absence almost cause a loss
But at the end—we regained our fame.

Looking back on the good old days
We thought they'd never end.
We had no wheels to call our own
But we got there—just the same.

Things were different when we were young
We surfed on the waves—not the web.
We spent cash, now it's plastic instead.
We tanned in the sun—not in beds.

We wore our rings just on our fingers
And never in our nose.
There were no tattoos on our bodies
A belt held up our clothes.

Without television or computers
We found plenty to do.
Parents and teachers kept us on track
Hours wasted were few.

We only had home phones—not iPhones
No cell phones to take along
And there weren't "ear buds" for our ears
Records played our songs.

We didn't twitter—but we jittered,
Jitterbugged—of course.
We had air-mail, instead of e-mail
A typewriter was our source.

Face book and texting were unheard of,
We spoke face to face.
Telegrams or telephones were the quickest
With nothing from outer space.

Now TiVo and Wii entertain us
Keep us glued to the set.
In our time, work or play controlled us
So simple—don't forget!

We'd like to be a fly on the wall
That's what we use to say
Security cameras and Skype
Make it possible today!

Only our pies contained blackberries
A tooth might be loose—not blue.
We brushed our teeth to keep them white
I'd not put one in my ear—would you?

Back then, contacts were made to reach people
Now they are for the eyes.
They are used to help you see better
Glasses can be denied.

Map compasses were used to travel
Now it is the GPS
Punch in your next destination
Heed the instructions and rest.

Our drugs consisted of aspirins,
Given by our mothers.
Nothing like some kids take today.
Our drink was Coke—no other.

Our language was strange to our parents
Hubba-hubba, and swoon
We said "dream boat," "Roger," and "Yuk"
We listened to Crosby croon.

Our music was soft and words were clear
Like "Bewitched" or "Harbor Lights"
Whether it was formal dances or sock hops
Made you want to dance all night.

Your memories have inspired me
Many teachers you recalled
Chapman, Howard, Fowler, Lindermann
Too many to name all.

My poem is getting quite lengthy,
As my stanzas verify.
Our memories of the good and simple life
In 1950 at Temple High.
August 19, 2009

Our Hope

The longest lane, must have a turning,
The darkest night gives place to day,
Somewhere bright stars are always burning,
Hope's rainbow spans the future way.

The worst storm has the quickest ending,
The dreariest winter heralds spring,
With sunshine, blossom fragrance, blending,
To bring new joy to everything.

The End

Made in USA - Kendallville, IN
1089912_9780982315866
04.23.2020 1122